I0813451

CIRCUMTRAUMA

JUMOKE VERISSIMO

COACH HOUSE BOOKS, TORONTO

first edition

Canada Council for the Arts
Conseil des Arts du Canada

Ontario

Published with the generous assistance of the Canada Council for the Arts and the Ontario Arts Council. Coach House Books also acknowledges the support of the Government of Canada through the Canada Book Fund and the Government of Ontario through the Ontario Book Publishing Tax Credit.

LIBRARY AND ARCHIVES CANADA CATALOGUING IN PUBLICATION

Title: Circumtrauma / Jumoke Verissimo.
Names: Verissimo, Jumoke, author
Identifiers: Canadiana (print) 20250232545 | Canadiana (ebook) 20250232596 | ISBN 9781552455128 (softcover) | ISBN 9781770568778 (EPUB) | ISBN 9781770568761 (PDF)
Subjects: LCGFT: War poetry.
Classification: LCC PR9387.9.V475 C57 2025 | DDC 821/.92—dc23

Circumtrauma is available as an ebook: ISBN 978 1 77056 877 8 (EPUB), ISBN 978 1 77056 876 1 (PDF)

Purchase of the print version of this book entitles you to a free digital copy. To claim your ebook of this title, please email sales@chbooks.com with proof of purchase. (Coach House Books reserves the right to terminate the free digital download offer at any time.)

PREFACE

I began researching the Nigeria-Biafra War (also known as the Nigerian Civil War) because I wanted answers on why the conflict has stayed on the bodies of even the unborn. How does one capture the unacknowledged pain that resonates across generations and may even inform the lens from which social relations are formed?

My attempting to translate this deeply felt conviction into a coherent and impactful work proved to be a daunting undertaking. There were the times of grappling with the ethical complexities of representing such sensitive experiences, struggling to find a narrative structure that would honour the multiplicity of voices without homogenizing their individual suffering. There were moments of profound uncertainty, where the weight of the stories threatened to overwhelm me. I questioned my own capacity to do justice to the magnitude of the subject, wrestling with the fear of perpetuating further misrepresentation or erasure.

Despite these challenges, the unwavering belief in the importance of this work, coupled with the invaluable support of mentors, collaborators, and those who generously shared their personal histories, propelled me forward. This project became a collective endeavour, a testament to the power of shared memory and the enduring human spirit. The book you hold in your hands is not solely my creation, but a culmination of countless acts of courage, empathy, and unwavering commitment. It testifies to the power of bearing witness, a fragile attempt to make meaning of the complexities of personal grief and public memory, and a humble offering toward understanding the enduring legacy of the war. In fact, the language of this collection is definitely unconventional and nothing like I have ever written. The poem that opens the collection, 'From Source to Scar,' employs the structure of code to explore the foundational layers of memory and the persistent algorithms of inherited pain. Consider it a different dialect, one where syntax and symbol bear witness alongside verse. I believe that within its structure lies an attempt to encode the very origins of this enduring pain. I therefore invite you to engage with its structure as you would the foundational code of a long-standing wound; see how its syntax embodies the very fractures and persistent patterns of memory. Understand how its syntax, in its very design, attempts to map the origins of inherited suffering. It is an exercise, perhaps, in learning to read beyond the familiar, a preparation for the profound act of witnessing the pain held within others' stories. This initial act of decipherment, like the rest of the poems in this collection, is an invitation: to attune yourself to the often-unconventional languages of pain and the profound need for our listening.

Jumoke Verissimo

OGBE: 2°

From Source to Scar

```
/*/
#include <past_country>        / / The weight of origin
#include <new_horizon>          / / The promise of arrival
#include <scars_carried>       / / Invisible wounds

using namespace memory;         / / The space where history resides

string warEcho = "departure -> arrival;"; / / A direct mapping of displacement

list<string> elderVoices = {    / / A collection of inherited narratives
    "shame_whispers",
    "strength_untold",
    "grief_unseen"
};

boolean healing = false;        / / The state of overcoming the past

while (!healing) {              / / An ongoing process
    int burden = elderVoices.count();
    int progress = random(0, 2); / / Erratic steps forward and then backward

    healing = (progress > burden / 3); / / A fragile tipping point
    burden--;                        / / The slow shedding of weight
}

class IdentityInTransit {       / / Defining self in movement
    string heritage = "diaspora_kin";
    option<string> rooted = maybe("rooted", "rootless"); / / The question
    of belonging

    boolean recognize(IdentityInTransit other) {
        return (this->heritage == other.heritage); // Shared history as
        recognition and then fractured
    }
}
```

```
function amplify(string story, int layers) { // The magnification of time
    return story + ("_echo" * layers);
}

IdentityInTransit us = new IdentityInTransit("seeking_ground");
IdentityInTransit them = new IdentityInTransit("building_anew");

if (us.recognize(them)) {
    print("kinship_acknowledged");
}   else {
    print("familiar_distance");
}

print(warEcho + "Healing:" + healing);
print("past_amplified:" + amplify("origin_trauma", 2));
print("future_uncertain");

// Does the code of our past ever truly stop running?
/*/
```

Program Output: the war ended: 4,000,000 stories still spend blood to live

oooo-b
oooo

| |
| |
| |
| |
naught

| |
| |
| |
| |
naught

| |
| |
| |
| |
naught*

1111-a
1111

our body is a people: before and after

our body is the fluent suffering of those who die lonely overseas
our body is   lying somewhere
our body is: a lonely home   an insanity
our body is a lake
our body is a flag   lying somewhere
our body is a room of suffering   a place for vandals to die
but the dead no longer suffer   but the dead have not apologized

but the dead have refuge   but the dead no longer suffer

our body is dead: women, children, and men without a name
our body   is a country running   without a head
blood is crying to remember
our blood is   crying to survive
our body is without a name
our body is a forest of threat/s   it is a history of blood
our body is without a name

1111-b
1111

our body is without a name
our body is a forest of threat/s   it is a history of blood

our blood is   crying to survive
blood is crying to remember

our body   is a country running   without a head
our body is the dead: women, children, and men without a name

but the dead have refuge   but the dead no longer suffer
but the dead no longer suffer   but the dead have not apologized

our body is a room of suffering   a place for vandals to die
our body is a flag   lying somewhere
our body is a lake

our body is: a lonely home   an insanity
our body is   lying somewhere
our body is the fluent suffering of those who die lonely overseas
our body is a people: before and after

1001-a
1001

after war
a mother and her family of four
        arrive in an airport taxi: a body of feudal songs

broken people   in dirty wrappers
        a fluent suffering body

we are of same material
our   body also collects feudal songs
before and after war   our body collects feudal songs

we know no sleep   we collect only fear.

1001-b
1001

we   know no sleep   we collect only fear.
before and after war   our body collects feudal songs
our   body also collects feudal songs
we are of same material

a fluent suffering body
broken   people   in dirty wrappers
arrive in an airport taxi: a body of feudal songs
a mother and her family of four
after war

0110-a
0110

a rickety train pulled up
heads disappeared
        our brothers left home
for a godforsaken place
        our brothers returned
with a gunshot in the head

0110-b
0110

with a gunshot in the head
our brothers returned

for a godforsaken place
our brothers left

heads disappeared
a rickety train pulled up

0011-a
0011

the sea cracked open
          and pushed out our past
to the end of the world

0011-b
0011

on night news:
we watched a rocket
in awkward silence

1100-a
1100

miles away.
he
called
i said:
please let's not fight
he stopped
realized what had happened

separated. i told
our friends,
i said please let's not fight
i stopped
miles away. friends here i realized what had happened. enemies there.

1100-b
1100

friends here. miles away. i realized what had happened. enemies there.
i stopped
i said please let's not fight
our friends,
separated. i told
realized what had happened
he stopped
please let's not fight
i said:
he
called
miles away.

0111-a
0111

everything was happening
as we were about to leave

flies
chirping bird
stampede

we didn't know
we were vandals.

0111-b
0111

we were vandals.
we didn't know

stampede

a chirping bird
flies
when we were about to leave
everything was happening

1110-a
1110

we thought we had rest – we thought we had victory
we thought we had planned ~~(full)~~ combat
to fight vandals of all kinds

no surrender, no surrender, no surrender to our enemy

they said we fought well
they slaughtered and we slaughtered
and they slaughtered
and we started to suffer from the slaughtered
and we fought hands together no surrender

later when our/their troops ran looking for citizens to kill
we hear: everyone is the enemy
everyone had victory

victory murmurs doubt

1110-b
1110

doubt is also peace
victory murmurs doubt

everyone had victory
we hear: everyone is the enemy
later when our/their troops ran looking for citizens to kill
and we fought hands together no surrender
and we started to suffer from the slaughtered
and they slaughtered
they slaughtered and we slaughtered
they said we fought well

no surrender, no surrender, no surrender to   our enemy
to fight vandals of all kinds
we thought we had a planned ~~(full)~~ combat

we thought we had rest – we thought we had victory

0001-a
0001

Black. wearing black. is wearing black. establishment is wearing black. the establishment is wearing black

0001-b
0001

the establishment is wearing black. establishment is wearing black. is wearing black. wearing black. black

1000-a
1000

the road was on fire
we did not stop for children

we have what to kill him
yes, all of us
not guns –

quietly, as he finished talking
laughed and hailed his friends
we started a song: to win the war

1000-b
1000

remember all the things we were speaking
everybody is the same
lusting after peace

i think of my mother red-eyed, wounded
hundred steps away from the centre

i begin to think
something would happen
perhaps. something would happen.

1011-a
1011

may we always remember to hear stories
of the laughing daughters who give flowers in a war

may we always remember crowded roads without room
may we understand anger of the gaunt and withdrawn ones
may we remember children with eyes like candlelit houses
the darkness that dabbed the country
the blackened vehicles and men in them
the silence of maxim guns, rapid-fire rifles
the sons who leave with nothing

may the enemy know we are not six miles away
may we know the enemy is not six miles away

1011-b
1011

may we know the enemy is *not* six miles away
may the enemy know we are *not* six miles away
may we always remember to hear stories
of the laughing daughters who give flowers in a war

may we always remember crowded roads without room
may we understand anger of the gaunt and withdrawn ones
may we remember children with eyes like candlelit houses
the darkness that dabbed the country

the sons who leave with nothing
the silence of maxim guns, rapid-fire rifles
the blackened vehicles and men in them
the silence of maxim guns, rapid-fire rifles

1101-a
1101

do paramount thoughts take place only in the west?

'like angry people are african/s –
those people will do anything – '

have the hunger shamed people
learnt hate is not a choice but a doing

like how to get ammunition to kill so many at a time
to hear shooting and turn away

like do not hear one another – tribal wars

like there is no room for smiling
when there is looted peace

we felt that way–
we felt our heart was not beating

but book people institute protest for property but not the home

1101-b
1101

mother died years ago she refused to come with us
now our house is the weight of empty
people have fled

our heart is beating saboteurs
the night is an army of fear

people are giving a lot of trouble
but god forbid that we should run

god we know a place can fall,   do we have to run.
we will come back   shamed

nothing one could do other than wait and hope
we are not safe   do we have to run.

what kind of thing is this, enough is enough
can we nurse hate in front of the house?

11
0100-a
0100

what kind of thing is this?
nobody is sure of anything
there was something wrong
another story under the moon

0100-b
0100

we were friends in the making
knacking tory under the moon[1]
when the plane landed
he refused to come with me

[1] Nigerian pidgin, it means telling stories under the moon

0010-a

she spoke as she had never spoken.
she was all arms and ammunition.

0010-b

every side of the story is a bridge
it is also a grave

0101-a
0101

about two months before the city actually fell
he watched his baby eat until oil grease was left on the plate
he dabbed at his nose. darkness descended on him, as he listened
to the gossips next door. he dropped the knife on the carpeted floor:
the river crossed to the farm and time occupied the town.

0101-b
0101

a man put the potato to boil after he gave his baby a bath
fear washed clean for when we are attacked at night
when men enter into the houses at night and fuck the women by force
nothing is good tonight. this very night. this night
we arranged three benches on the veranda to die.

1010-a
1010

blood like plastic flowers decorates the front of our house/s.
the government is silent there is plenty trouble
home is madness we have/had to run.

blood like plastic flowers decorates the front of our house/s.
we go abroad for peace
abroad *is* refuge
but we are the intruder

we are shamed silently
where do we derive peace?

we cannot *byforce*[2] anybody to like us

1010-b
1010

the war may have ended
but every life is still riddled with bullet holes,
some large, others small some missing

truth is like missing bullets
the government
holds the gun
come to us
with a big lie
and hear our sobs sometimes.

we listen, we know the country is a battlefield teaching faith.

---

[2] Pidgin English, which means influencing people by power or force to do something.

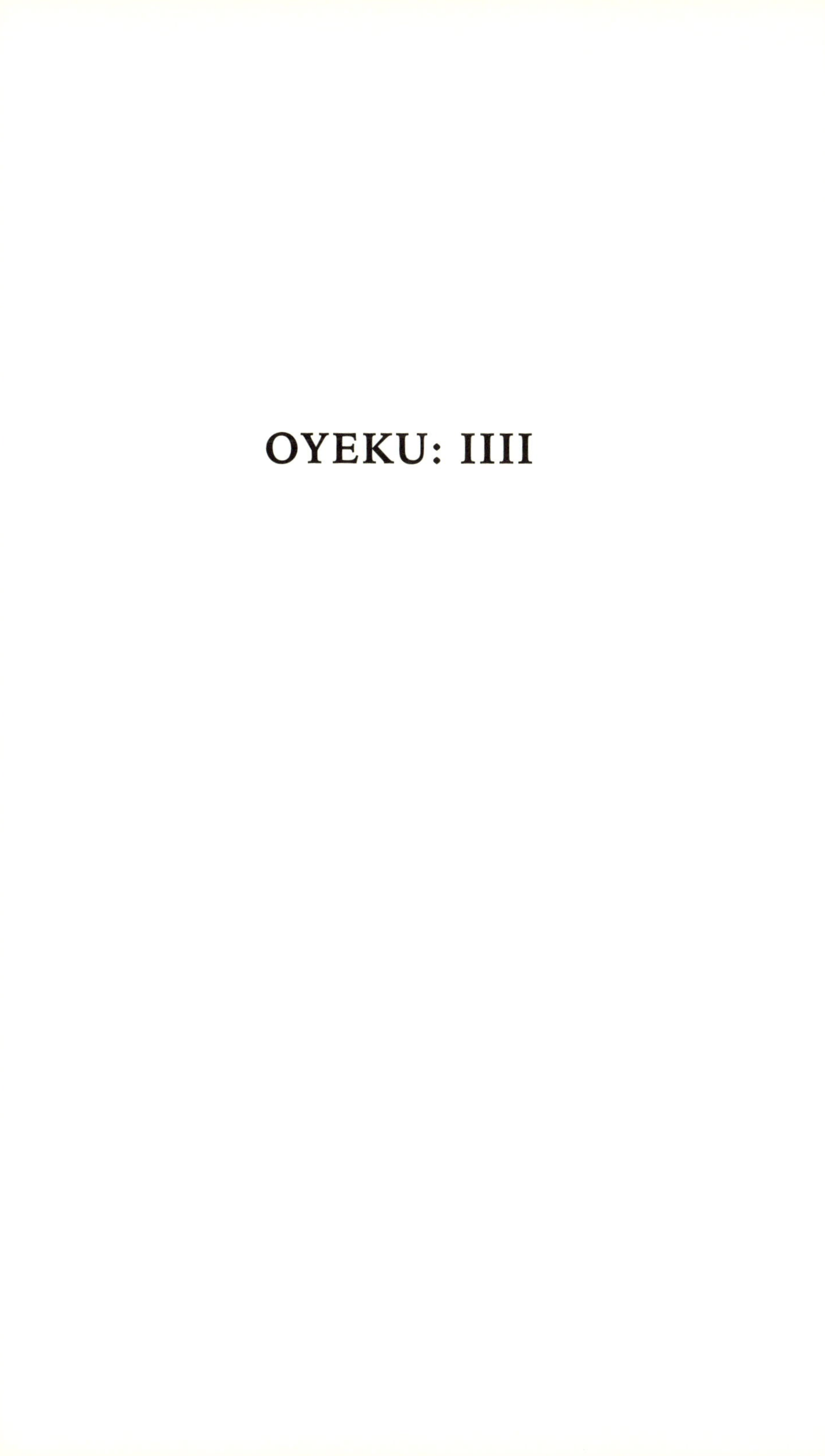

OYEKU: IIII

delete cat;
delete bird;
delete plants;
delete earth;
delete water = cleans::all_of(it);
/ / delete man;

cat = NULL;
bird = NULL;
plants = NULL;
earth = NULL;
water_that_cleans::all_of(it) = NULL;
/ / us = NULL;

---

the cat dies/the bird dies/the plants die/the earth dies
                                                                even water that cleans it all   dies
                                        yet we pray: may we not hear the death of us

10101010-a

i said nothing
|| || || ||

i said nothing
|| || || ||

i said nothing
|| || || ||

10101010-b

morning post
back to back
war to continue
at the centre
back
perhaps
to collect
trembling
saboteurs
an invading army
fighting
vandals

they will die to the last man

an invading army
we will starve to death.

01010101-a

there was no fighting
two men stood at the centre
waiting to be shot

the original son
with patches of night under the armpits
wanted to cross the enemy lines
to get the *foto*[3]
of his dead parents
he started to look at the pictures
                    determined
all set for battle
he talked to his mother
he talked to his father

there was silence
there was hate.

01010101-b

i said nothing
|| || || ||

i said nothing
|| || || ||

i said nothing
|| || || ||

---

[3] 'Photo' in pidgin English. Ken Saro-Wiwa's novel *Sozaboy* is written in what he describes as 'rotten English,' and when these words are used in the cut-up poem I leave them as it is.

10000010-a

refugees
|| || || ||

refugees
|| || || ||

refugees
|| || || ||

10000010-b

he talked to my father
luckily, he was calm
his name was isaac
his friends are dead

he was talking like planes landing and taking off
i smelt the harsh pain on his breath

he will not marry me
with that superior smile of people who were born
to hold arms and ammunitions to fight –

01000001-a

we all wanted to be shot – seeing
bodies   everywhere
we could surrender   and die

the pistol is the hand   the stage
the grip   the fingers

the threat of peace

tattered-looking and hungry people
  see themselves as ready food.

you people forget   death came before the bullet.

01000001-b

refugees
|| || || ||

refugees
|| || || ||

refugees
|| || || ||

00101000-a

astretchofsilence astretchofsilence astretchofsilence
|| || || ||
                    astretchofsilence astretchofsilence astretchofsilence
|| || || ||
astretchofsilence astretchofsilence astretchofsilence
|| || || ||

00101000-b

street. sand. salt. a drink.
hurricane smoke come to an agreement
nobody should be a stretch of silence

slack mouth clutch at mortality
anti-aircraft somebody

words comforted   not for long

00010100-a

the awning of the veranda nourished our questions
with bodies dumped outside the airport lounge
we watched the dead listen to members of the 'War cabinet'
say, god is always on the side of guns, guns – and arms
like clumps of dry air that eat infants' mouths

the awning of the veranda nourished our questions
when they told us run to the barracks and we did not.

00010100-a

astretchofsilence astretchofsilence astretchofsilence
|| || || ||
astretchofsilence astretchofsilence astretchofsilence
|| || || ||
astretchofsilence astretchofsilence astretchofsilence
|| || || ||

00001010-a

sorrow
|| || || ||
sorrow
|| || || ||
sorrow
|| || || ||

00001010-a

the more we kill the more
many would die quick-quick
in the not too distant future

00000101-a

why is the world
we live in
like an automatic pistol

00000101-a

sorrow
|| || || ||
sorrow
|| || || ||
sorrow
|| || || ||

10100000-a

frightened
|| || || ||
frightened
|| || || ||
frightened
|| || || ||

10100000-b

her arms wrapped around herself
she sat on the dining table like a statue

they made her feel inconsequential
holy and desecrated and abused

though there was no air raid
there was a massacre

she was begging them not to father
that her children were the message

the house became empty
virtually empty

his 'work harder'
sounded like massacres.

01010000-a

in front of the embassy
she had a dream but did not remember
                                        what it was
her friend was working feverishly
                                        in new york
the weather conditions organized
the people into refugees in the school hall

please feel at home
although everything is in fragments

please feel at home
don't remember you are starving

tears filled her eyes as she turned to go

01010000-b

frightened
|| || || ||
frightened
|| || || ||
frightened
|| || || ||

00101010-a

fight
|| || || ||
        fight
        || || || ||
                fight
                || || || ||

00101010-b

they said self-sufficiency is dying
they asked us to leave

for theirs is the kingdom of heaven
their god is very powerful

we have just run from the hole
we crossed the river to the farm
our way home is middle-aged

00010101-a

all of them attacking us
shouting 'fire' if we leave

silence thickened our saliva
we cannot defend our children
when trouble come

uncertainty is a bomb
we do not want to die like chickens.

00010101-b

fight
|| || || ||
fight
|| || || ||
fight
|| || || ||

10101000-a

run empty-handed
|| || || ||
run empty-handed
|| || || ||
run empty-handed
|| || || ||

10101000-b

they talked about care for the tribe
as if there was something else they knew
that we did not

like a stranger
we went in search of accommodation
they fought us every night.

for many nights when they came
they stole everything in the house
but we did not know why

after these encounters
if they were coming
we don't run, we do not fight again

we are *the* minority group
we live knowing they killed our people.

01010100-a

the oil cleared our throats
after all, we go to war fronts to die

moist bodies close the darkness
astringent scent of *politicians* drew near

the war had changed everyone
maybe there might be an exception

stretched legs occupied benches
eat body parts like they did in congo

i believe we are not going to run
even if anything happens. don't worry

don't worry about all these things
they have not left though they are packing

we would take hardship and go out
in the streets singing the last hymn of peace

01010100-b

run empty-handed
|| || || ||
run empty-handed
|| || || ||
run empty-handed
|| || || ||

00000010-a

surrender
|| || || ||
surrender
|| || || ||
surrender
|| || || ||

00000010-b

why don’t you do something/ why don’t you do something/ why don’t
you do something/ why don’t you

000000001-a

you left us nothing. you left us nothing. you left us. nothing. you left. you left us nothing.

000000001-b

surrender
|| || || ||
surrender
|| || || ||
surrender
|| || || ||

1001: IWORI

A Soldier's Journal

Inside a.out:

```
00002000  01 00 02 00 00 00 00 00  00 00 00 00 00 00 00 00  |The boy's name      |
00002010  74 68 65 20 62 6f 79 e2  80 99 73 20 6e 61 6d 65  |was Samuel, fr-     |
00002020  20 77 61 73 20 73 61 6d  75 65 6c 2c 20 66 72 6f  |om degema, so       |
00002030  6d 20 64 65 67 65 6d 61  20 61 6e 64 20 73 6f 20  |young you could     |
00002040  79 6f 75 6e 67 20 79 6f  75 20 63 6f 75 6c 64 20  |see unbroken        |
00002050  73 65 65 20 75 6e 62 72  6f 6b 65 6e 20 79 65 61  |years stretched     |
00002060  72 73 20 61 68 65 61 64  20 6f 66 20 68 69 6d 2e  |ahead of him. I     |
00002070  0a 69 20 6e 61 6d 65 64  20 68 69 6d 20 73 6d 61  |named him smallie   |
00002080  6c 6c 69 65 2c 20 74 68  65 20 6e 6f 74 65 70 61  |The notepad I       |
00002090  64 20 69 20 77 72 69 74  65 20 74 68 69 73 20 66  |write this from     |
000020a0  72 6f 6d 20 69 73 20 6d  61 64 65 20 66 72 6f 6d  |is made from        |
000020b0  20 68 75 6d 61 6e 20 73  6b 69 6e 2e 0a 69 20 61  |human skin. I       |
000020c0  6d 20 6e 6f 77 20 75 73  65 64 20 74 6f 20 77 72  |am now used to      |
000020d0  69 74 69 6e 67 20 77 69  74 68 20 74 68 65 20 62  |writing             |
000020e0  6c 6f 6f 64 20 6f 66 20  6d 65 6e 20 77 68 6f 20  |with the blood      |
000020f0  63 61 6e 6e 6f 74 20 64  69 65 2c 20 62 75 74 20  |of men who          |
00002100  68 65 72 65 20 69 20 66  65 65 6c 20 73 6f 6d 65  |cannot die, but     |
00002110  74 68 69 6e 67 20 6c 69  6b 65 20 6f 6e 65 20 66  |here I feel some    |
00002120  65 65 6c 20 6e 6f 74 68  69 6e 67 3a 0a 00 00 00  |-thing akin to      |
00002130  00 00 00 00 00 00 00 00  74 68 65 20 77 61 79 20  |feel nothing: the   |
00002140  74 68 65 20 74 6f 6e 67  75 65 20 68 6f 6c 64 73  |way the tongue      |
00002150  20 68 75 6d 61 6e 20 73  70 69 72 69 74 2c 20 6c  |holds human         |
00002160  6f 6f 73 65 20 61 6e 64  20 79 65 74 20 67 72 6f  |spirit, loose and   |
00002170  75 6e 64 65 64 3b 0a 74  68 65 72 65 e2 80 99 73  |yet grounded.       |
00002180  20 73 6f 6d 65 74 68 69  6e 67 20 61 62 6f 75 74  |There's some-       |
00002190  20 74 68 65 20 73 6b 69  6e 20 6f 66 20 61 20 64  |thing about the     |
000021a0  65 61 64 20 6d 61 6e 2e  0a 69 20 63 6f 75 6c 64  |skin of a dead      |
000021b0  20 66 69 6e 64 20 61 20  77 61 79 20 74 6f 20 73  |man. I could        |
000021c0  61 79 20 75 6e 65 76 65  6e 2c 20 62 75 74 20 68  |find a way to       |
000021d0  6f 77 20 64 6f 20 79 6f  75 20 73 61 79 20 64 65  |describe it as      |
000021e0  61 64 20 74 6f 20 61 20  73 6b 69 6e 20 67 61 73  |uneven, but how     |
000021f0  70 69 6e 67 20 6f 6e 20  79 6f 75 72 20 66 69 6e  |you pronounce       |
00002200  67 65 72 2c 20 73 70 65  61 6b 69 6e 67 3b 20 69  |dead to a skin      |
00002210  20 61 6d 20 68 65 72 65  3b 0a 00 00 00 00 00 00  |gasping on your     |
00002220  00 00 00 00 00 00 00 00  6b 69 6c 6c 20 6d 65 20  |finger, speaking    |
00002230  6f 6e 63 65 3b 0a 72 61  69 73 65 20 61 20 6d 75  |I am here; kill     |
```

```
00002240  6c 74 69 74 75 64 65 3f  0a 00 00 00 01 1b 03 3b   |me once; raise    |
00002250  88 00 00 00 10 00 00 00  d4 ed ff ff bc 00 00 00   |a multitude       |
00002260  14 ee ff ff e4 00 00 00  24 ee ff ff fc 00 00 00   |..................?................|
```

Output:

The boy's name was Samuel, from Degema, so young you could see unbroken years stretched ahead of him. I named him smallie. The notepad I write this from is made from human skin. I am now used to writing with the blood of men who cannot die, but here I feel something akin to feeling nothing: the way the tongue holds human spirit, loose and yet grounded. There's something about the skin of a dead man. I could find a way to describe it as uneven, but how do you pronounce dead to a skin gasping on your finger, speaking: I am here; kill me once; raise a multitude?

11010111-a

we are an angry body
collector of corpses clutching a spoon smeared with blood

old, young, men and women turning into angry artillery soldiers
a city of moving corpses

silence is furtive freedom
hate is fear in a tent
we are a body sprawled in groan
we are moving corpses: women and children and men

home is a collector of weeping
morning is for blood debt
night is reserved for thinking
our world is smeared in blood

we are bones and
we tell them we want out
we are angry   we tell them we want out we tell them we are out.

11010111-a

bia nwanyi! [4]
Woman,   every day you find angry black scorpions
among your friends.

Woman,   no time for work. no time for peace.
no time to be happy.
no time, except   for hate.

Woman,
you can't keep imagining happy in your country
we can see   you are not happy at all.

---

[4] 'Come, woman' in Igbo language.

11101011-a

go   fight   let the young people die
abandon the oppressed
know   if you kill them   they will return

I don't think anybody can help
the oppressed
but know   if you kill them   they will return

don't you see?   all that
that there was always   oppression
if you kill them   twenty-one times   they will return
fodder for the evening news   unreal
here and go fight   for the oppressed

11101011-b

they are: a people dedicated to the cause
of resentment

resigned
disappointed
low   voices
worry   from the confrontation
the implications
of being alone with their body
their broken body

01111101-a

our fears are old
        and languid
our fears are old pawns
        in their hands
our fears
        run a few errands
for some of us
to die awake

when it is time
for us to die
        we clean off mud
silently and sorrowfully
        take our bullets of suffering
without being seen

01111101-b

a pregnant woman set a church on fire
we pick up hope to see if
death and life
lap all the time
but raw pain
won't send hate away

10111110-a

slowly
wait and plan
plan and control
every day
plan and wait and control
every day   to movc vandals

10111110-b

we were all brothers
massacred
albeit   on a very small scale

we are all memory's children
superior in our pain

our guests hold their noses
heads against the table
eyes turned away
driven into the evening
of our pain

we fear anything
with the photo
of tattered battle dress

01011111-a

you must   come   with us
                        trusting
redemptive   anticipation of God's help

you must   come   with us
        along another footpath
trusting
        a philandering peace
trusting   us not to fight
        or sin against the scriptures
trusting
that
with   a wounded shoulder
you will not leave
the town
                angry

01011111-b

the world news:
we watched a rocket
in awkward silence

10101111-a

we are not going to run
at the slightest hint of criticism
even with the sun sweating

10101111-b

gossip time is precious
but we did not understand one another's language
and everyone left the town at first concern
even the cemetery was empty of bodies
but I'll rather die here

I feel like dying
exhausted from fear
it is cold bitterness
to live the miserable life of old clothes

I know the gramophone pain
of a street that frightened the dark
where the band, their singers sang contempt
in a voice strong and never defeated

I shall go out and practise
how to die without bitterness

11110101-a

He knew us
He knew us and more
He said we were cowards

i. Cowards will be interpreted
By each moment

ii. Cowards murdered Enugu, murdered Onitsha
You murdered villages –
And without ammunition

iii. Cowards receive visitors
Who uprooted and destroyed us all
Left us no food to eat
And deserted years before
While we await evacuation

iv. Your people. All your people
Are evil. Cowards.

11110101-b

one morning
he said   my son
the War
the farm
the ammunition
is inside   me

my memory
is
a
little
boy
a stranger is looking through me

11101010-a

a young man came up to our house
rich and influential
said to my mother
the door for the returned is a road
to be forgotten

I have returned   tarnished
exhausted
run over like a bush rat that leapt
from a tree

in the civil service
        the civilians
never had a chance

11101010-b

my husband said
that in war we count the dead   and
cemetery targets people's beds, invading sleep

he says, rain would have destroyed us all
like water entering our noses   and we can't breathe
but we got flowers in bullet holes instead

he says, me tell you, you can't live
when all your people.
drown in tears
you will not float

he says, they did not send us rain
but rain would have destroyed us all

0111111-a

everybody is afraid
things continue as before
but we are not going to run
we stay and die
cutting their hand or their legs

maybe
we are going to run
for there is always hope
peace is staged
in western europe and america

put it down in anger
run along i'll bury love

defend kinsmen
defend our fatherland
carrying a heavy load on the head

0111111-b

returning defenders arms in the air
armed soldier
soldier combing –

arms in the air
infiltrators

the past will not believe
our life and death were numbers

10111111-a

the enemy is time
since she was a child

from the earliest days
time rose and fell
gathering standstorm
gathering standstorm in the distance

because nothing is forgotten

10111111-b

the walls are broken
we have nothing for you
to defend our children
they mustn't cry blood as tears
to see clearly

we left as spirits
nothing at all to alarm anybody
that we lost our eyes
that we can't be ourselves
accommodate the swell of our fears
we curse the lucky soldiers
love the sons more
protect the people
who live by forgetting

for the rebellion
is to remember
and not voice a defeat

11111101-a

hate is important too
for corpses walking
moving with men
for sons
meeting skeletons
to battle love
for men combing
the smoke for rooms

the dying trying to tell
of home of sons of women
of doors
and a body

buried in prayers and a hymn

Jesus wept?

11111101-b

we have arms superior weapons come to us
we have plastered blood in villages
we have arms and soldiers in big black boots saying –
your children are safe

yourchildrenaresafe *is*
the erasing of memory

this saying – your children are safe by the army
is erasing (our) memory

send us to see whether villages are dancing to the gun
and we will rest hate

we will cut tomorrow up, for
bloodblood
blood can set us free
blood is the government of our fatherland/blood is the property we
hold for money
blood

is erasing (our) memory

1111110-a

all had been taken from the fatherland
red-stained flies buzzed everywhere
things packed for children   were behind

god ended her   she was at peace
bury her   bury her past
    bury the past
    for a long time

intruder   deserter
enemy   friend
cursing and smiling at each other
    killing though the cruel War was over

hate is a heavy load
    all had been taken
but we carry resentment along

1111110-b

war is a question of practice
the mercenary is there
the soldier is there
the children, women ...
all there to wash the blood away

rocket shall come like rainstorms
every man and woman
will practise fleeing

and manoeuvre in private
how to go out   without hating

love is ~~not~~ important to writers
who report war and its many practices

when there is an important fight
love is only an art
where we can become frantic
about practice

01010111-a

ravaged town
an embassy gate won't open
broken women statue
dead people: a small crowd made of cement
shit in a trouser
a broken car
a body by the bush
packed and forgotten children's things
bloodstained rag wound
dead teen soldier
warm body of a child turning cold
friends left behind
no farm to run to
broken trees crying
        this is how yesterday returns

01010111-b

memory is famished

10101011-a

how do you feel
            a fierce emboldening rage
rage standing like a rundown hut

doing sorrow alone is
handed down hatred
held down   ashes
an illiterate rage
            clustered water droplets
that won't heal a sapped root

            how do you feel?
bearing tales of bullets
splattered with holes
a pistol   in the head
as the prayers before meal.

10101011-b

a modest life without blood.   A life   without   blood
is
a pistol

11010101-a

they wept
shoulders touching   each night

they reviewed their situation
frustration everywhere
we did this
we did this to ourselves

why stay and die
as criminals
in this river of blood

we are all casualties
they are muscles and no brain
no readiness to apologize

we all are people
with nowhere else to go
like the last verse of a hymn

11010101-b

big mama was going
with us
tears filled her eyes as she   turned to go
she remembered   *that* running   headless body clearly
in front   of the embassy
our fear   as large   as the sky
when the foreign voice on radio said it was   *just* a tribal War
but that's not   how we remember the dead

11101010-a

a shot was heard
you cut his hand
run empty-handed

wares behind
his hand appears again
holding an automatic pistol

what did he do? I ask you
you remember nothing

11101010-b

we are exhausted
tomorrow is for independence
away from suffering independence

in these uncertainties
young men buying guns
to attack and kill one another
calling for a takeover
provided unfinished knowledge

brain like cement
they disappear down the road
to get rid of the vandals

it is worrying
those casualties
of the massacres
ask for independence
and get same old fight

0110: ODI

```
#include <iostream>
#include <vector>
using namespace std;

// Handed down
class GenerationsPast {};
class Stories: public GenerationsPast {
  public:
    Stories() {}
    Stories(char* newStory) {}
};
void us(Stories words, Stories letters) {};
bool _(vector<string> stories) {
  for (string story : stories) {
    cout << story << endl;
  }
  return false;
}

int main() {
  #define words
  do {
    words
      _({"squish",
      "hope into fragile pulps",
      "of misery"});
  } while (
    _({"they leave the tongue in the twilight of despair",
    "in the dawn",
    "of sorrow"})
  );
  #define words
  Stories before_we_utter_them, before_we_collect;
  us(before_we_utter_them, before_we_collect);
```

```
   class InstructionsInSurvival: public Stories {
      Stories* fate = new Stories("decided upon before arrival");
   };
}
```

Program Output:
before thcy/leave the tongue
in the twilight/of despair
in the dawn/of sorrow
do words squish/hope into fragile pulps/of misery
is this about/what words mean inside us
before we utter them/before we collect
them into stories/instructions in survival
handed down
to the generation
next
to their fate/
decided upon
before they arrived.

01101001-a

what were they searching   for
her face   slick with fear's sweat
perhaps it was worth it   to let her
be a saucer
        flying
with loud gasps   choking
from dirt of freedom and oppression
the weary bustle of
pleasing and angering
her friends at the same time

01101001-b

there was no danger   to convince him
to question   to answer
to think
about secession
about a new country
expecting peace

10010110-a

are you ready for trouble?
you have spoken
                    enough
asking for help from
the heads supplying
                    pain and blood

10010110-b

we have lost our freedom
nothing private anymore
the house   is standing
on dissolving grounds

their apology
is a bucket of ash

our people count shattered nerves
all our friends are dead

we have enemies and freedom

01001011-a

anything
chopping small-small people
massacres all conversations
    where we talk about tomorrow

stilted
    silence in the middle of a conversation
tell me how people count hollowness

an interest bordered
    with a gunfight

01001011-b

I always dreamt they came
dead
daughters, sons, fathers, mothers
with a hollow middle

10000111-a

who goes to another man
to pull out their penis
and insert it into a book

who goes to another man
to pull out their penis
and insert it into a gun

10000111-b

i remember my life of sorrow
i don't remember my dreams of freedom
they are not identical

11100001-a

violent words arrived
                    on the streets
and aged peace
          then the street became
an angry place
          our throat: hard-soft cartilage
          lacking words
blames strolled, sidestep responsibility
and left no next of kin

11100001-b

the ally. was cold
the plan did not ask
who would leave dead
thirty-six months equals waste
not time.
limp. command. kept
disbelief. always option is
war. report. provoke
loss. night. unlock
time
and unending shame or hate or pain.

110110010-a

who is going to resist them?
        is it bitterness

quick   quick
        quick slow   belly slow
refugee camp   bitterness
        painfully ridiculous

idiot smile bitterness
we were defeated
                bitterness
        set up and work them
believe us   believe them
the courageous ones   who leave

110110010-b

fire razed down books
cement figure clapped hands
huge dark shadows
razing children
opening a
history of silence
to speak disdain
to be open
to trouble everywhere

011011011-a

remember
the first sign
of goodbye

tiptoed across
unfolded
and folded

we are lost
so much now
it will not happen again

011011011-b

pause
something calcified
how can
the world not end?
damn saboteurs
causing panic
to fight again

have they forgotten
we haven't healed?

10010111-a

strong campaign
of evils
lead us to other beginnings

forced very far away
hurried back
peace isn't there
peace isn't home

10010111-b

disgrace spread like wildfire
mingling the outside
into insane nights
meeting empty mornings

our new peace left for a place
about to fall

don't you see us evacuating?

11010110-a

her ancestors don't forgive
their stories don't forget
how
        their hearts splintered
        they were killing them
like ants

        a meaningless ragged bazaar
to hide anybody with stories.

11010110-b

they are here
clawing one another
vehement about it
i did not know
there was nothing
we could do about it

heavy lips labour
saying our world
will soon end

all this hunting
running
can make you lame

they are there
they are here

11010110-a

I am going to forbid
the land of my birth
where people are running from
because
they wished
the whole War thing over
the ground yelled and yelled
shouted at the legs
on the ground
huts turned into bushes
radio walking
up and down
trigger calamity
this country is the problem

11010110-b

we have come for combing
they come every night
fuck the women   force
force the women   fuck

i want to protect her from harm
from hunger all her life
i have no other choice
i must die
i am not man
if i have to die, why not now?

01000011-a

I cannot understand at all
the huge problem of land
when the crisis came
we were all there
            waiting and waiting
for our country the vandal
            to arrive
it left us nothing
so many of us are gone

01000011-b

We never dream of driving a silver cloud

10000011-a

a missing heading

10000011-b

I have no alternative
Cursing
Grumble
Cursing
Remain behind them

False tooth
False smile
False friends
give you trouble

11000001-a

All was not well
There was no evil he did not excel
Every member of the family
Hijacked the road
Stowed the ash
Demonstrated how to make friends

A hundred steps
Something was wrong somewhere
They had no notion of what we had gone through

11000001-b

two friends
returned
holding hands
for a fraction of a second
there was a distance
as the mercenaries
came out for cover
in a rumpled black dress

11000010-a

grief made her helpless
brought the urge
to stretch
her pain
to worry about time

she did not trust her friends
they know her stories of guns
hours to have target shooting

11000010-b

he broke the silence:
why is she here
with forgotten lines
of a shot bomber
and his stories

nothing is happening
over time and space
a single act could reverberate
austere emptiness
tomorrow wants to sleep

11001011-a

we began to run
my father and mother
they could have made it
i cannot forget

i heard my name
i refused to save her people
their reaction
rants and impassioned articles

a brave man cannot die for an enemy

11001011-b

trouble in the country
cost blood

our father's house
is a quiet pool of blood
rumpled skin   spurts of –
seceded dreams

it was the way
it should be
to keep guard
to remember
liberated selfishness

11000111-a

they were merciful
but we have not come here
to answer questions

and dreams of blurred territory
  cnjoying
  our emotional problems

we are threatened
  once in a while
like they opened fire on us

how can it end
  how can it end when –

11000111-b

They are different
We are different
They are different
We are different
They are different
We are different
They are different

That is the problem.

METHOD NOTE, OR CIRCLING THE WOUNDING

Wherever we go, whoever we become, in each step we carry our stories.

I. A TWEET, A TIKTOK, AND A LINGERING WAR

The passing of Queen Elizabeth II sparked widespread commentary, but it was a controversial tweet by a Nigerian American professor, accusing the queen of complicity in the genocide against the Igbo people during the Nigerian Civil War, that particularly caught my attention, sharply highlighting the enduring impact of that conflict. For many like me who did not witness the war, the stories from elders, fiction, and history books were how we learnt about the war. As of today, the war is no longer taught in schools, due to the exclusion of history lessons. In fact, generations younger than mine only came to actively know about the war following novels like Chimamanda Ngozi Adichie's *Half of a Yellow Sun*.

The thing about history books, however, is that they will always miss the raw stories, the civilian scars, the yawning ache that remains. These untold narratives, how we grapple with stories of loss, are key. That tweet, sharp and brief, revealed how these wounds are still raw. Today, the Igbo remain the most aggrieved, as they claimed to have lost the greatest number of citizens, and their collective dream. There are also the minority ethnic groups, who were caught in the crossfire of the major sides, unsure of how to capture their own victimhood. The Federal side's narrative was that it needed to go to war with the seceding Biafrans because it was important to defend the nation from collapsing, hence they shouldn't be considered as villians.

It is therefore understandable that every mention of the war creates a ripple that questions the foundation of what we call Nigeria.

Nigeria is a country with over 250 ethnic groups; the Hausa, Igbo, and Yoruba are considered the major ones. In the history books, the

Nigeria-Biafra War (1967–70) began when the largely Igbo southeastern region of Nigeria, known as Biafra, declared independence. History books say that in response to this declaration by the new state, the Nigerian federal government launched a military campaign to prevent the secession. The books go on to provide historical context, highlighting the war along with its entanglement with the legacy of colonialism (Nigeria had ceased to be a British colony only in 1960). However, these official narratives often fall short of capturing the visceral experiences of civilian suffering and the enduring emotional and psychological trauma, leaving a significant gap in our understanding of the conflict's true cost. These suppressed narratives, including how we receive, acknowledge, or contest stories of massacres and starvation, are vital for a complete understanding of the conflict's legacy.

The professor's controversial tweet, despite the brevity that Twitter imposes, found a way to accentuate the ongoing contestation of historical narratives and the deep-seated wounds that persist among many Nigerians following the war. This persistence of old divisions, even across time and platforms, became even clearer to me during another stage of finalizing the poems in *Circumtrauma*.

The reach of the war's enduring impact became apparent in a shocking incident: a Canadian Nigerian posted a TikTok video threatening to poison the food of Nigerian colleagues from a different ethnic group, a reaction seemingly rooted in reciprocal online hate. This incident underscored how these old divisions and inherited violence continue to shape identity and social relations, even far from Nigeria.

These moments underscored the war's persistent grip, a conflict 'ended' on paper yet alive in the people, moving with Nigerians as they move. This led me to grapple with a fundamental question that became the heart of *Circumtrauma*: What do you do with a memory that feels like a story, but isn't quite, yet lives within?

II. RESENTMENT BEYOND BORDERS

War's shadows are long. Displacement isn't just leaving a place; it's a disruption of time, leaving people in a state of limbo. Lives become layered with old stories, bound to past grievances. These inherited burdens of negative emotion, carried by survivors, are the lingering manifestation of war's unresolved trauma, a persistent and potentially volatile undercurrent. Lives become entangled in these narratives of pain, creating cycles of recurring hurt. War's true story overflows the boundaries of history books. So many voices yearn to be heard, some loud, some silenced. History books will only ever offer just a glimpse. The limitations of historical accounts mean that the war's true legacy lies in these deeply personal, often unspoken stories, passed down through generations and carried across borders, fuelling resentment and hindering a conflictless future. If books cannot feel, this means the unborn will carry the weight forward.

Consequently, the haunting legacy of the war lies in the inherent impossibility of fully capturing its intricacies, leaving us with a burden of untold stories and a collective ache that fragments any vision of a peaceful future. After war, a cacophony of stories emerges, each filtered through the teller's role. Perhaps the 'end' of the war merely institutionalized the existing hate, so these unwritten narratives continue to divide, even beyond borders.

III. FINDING A NEW FORM: LISTENING FOR THE UNSPOKEN

Recognizing the limitations of traditional historical accounts and academic analyses in fully conveying the lived experience of the war and its lasting emotional impact, *Circumtrauma* seeks a new form to explore these neglected dimensions. While traditional approaches to understanding the war have focused on areas like historiography, identity formation, and trauma representation, they often fall short of fully capturing its enduring emotional legacy on Nigerian society. Our inclination to create coherent war narratives contrasts sharply with the surging and receding nature of inherited pain, which resists equilibrium.

As I researched, I realized we needed to create space for these stories and acknowledge the war's enduring impact on Nigerian society. We need to let these stories find new spaces, even if they are uncomfortable. My central aim in shaping *Circumtrauma* was to give voice to the raw, negative emotions often overlooked in dominant war narratives, emotions that reveal how a supposedly resolved conflict continues to fuel division. While *Circumtrauma* centres on the Nigerian war, the broader truth that emerges is how the lingering emotional resonance of conflict, as seen in Nigeria, reveals stories as potent weapons used to shape future narratives. How is it that we do not even realize how many seeds of resentment are sown in the fertile soil of hate, dividing and polarizing social groups beyond the years of the war?

IV. A CHORUS OF BORROWED VOICES: THE CUT-UP AS DIVINATION

Because the war is remembered in fractured and diverse ways, I sought a space for multiple voices to resonate, recognizing the power and the demand of the many conflicting narratives surrounding the war. Because my work had already begun in the direction of literary analysis, among the materials I was working with, I resolved to engage with Nigeria-Biafra War novels. My background in literary analysis led me to four key books: Chimamanda Ngozi Adichie's *Half of a Yellow Sun*, Flora Nwapa's *Never Again*, Ken Saro-Wiwa's *Sozaboy*, and Kole Omotoso's *The Combat*. These offered diverse perspectives on the war. I used them as emotional maps, source texts to tap into the raw feelings within their narratives.

My selection is based on the negative emotional currents of ethnic rivalry, disunity, and class. Each novel layers its own viewpoint. War novels often look back with sorrow, seeking to voice the silenced. Aiming to generate new meanings and capture the war's complexity, I sought to create a literary space deeply embedded within the emotional world of these novels, using their own language. I wanted to inhabit the emotional narrative of a past generation, their unresolved trauma.

I knew I needed their words to speak to each other, alongside the words of those whose stories have not yet been written. My initial poems felt too much like my own echo. My methodology combined cut and mixed extracts from the novels with oral and digital war remembrance stories to forge poetry that reflects the intensity of emotions and reveals the cyclical nature of the war's trauma. As I pieced these extracts together, the underlying violence began to emerge. But something was missing: a way to give form to this fractured language, to explore the negative emotions we carry. This process of weaving together fragmented texts with oral accounts resonated with the oral tradition inherent in Ifá, a significant divination system. In Ifá, a vast body of oral verses (*Odu Ifá*) contains ancient wisdom and stories. These verses are accessed and understood through a complex system of pattern interpretation that emerges during divination. Acquiring the skill for interpretation requires years of training and attention. However, the reliance on discerning meaning from patterns within the oral tradition is central to how Ifá has been transmitted and continues to offer insights across generations. This pattern-based approach to understanding deeply resonated with my own process of rearranging the fragmented language of the war novels. My belief that rearrangement could force new stories and reveal hidden meanings aligns with Mary Frances's observation: 'Any re-arrangement of objects, images or text insists that we tell ourselves alternative stories, that we ask new questions'. This principle guided my use of the cut-up, combined with oral stories, in what I call a vocalege, as a way of listening for the unspoken, a process akin to how divination systems like Ifá interpret patterns to understand the present and future. Inspired by this logic, I made divination the guiding framework for shaping the book.

V. THE WOUND THAT LINGERS: THE NEED FOR A NEW LANGUAGE

Circumtrauma explores the fundamental emotional dimension that shapes war narratives, revealing how this affective power defines and affects our social interactions. It tries to capture how war narratives are held together by an underlying valence that defines and affects our social interactions. It is about how trauma persists, creating ongoing conditions of pain, and becomes a proximate emotion, waiting to be triggered. The unacknowledged negative emotions of the war fuel a cycle where traumatic memories build and resurface, perpetuating the conditions of *Circumtrauma*. My aim, while not thematic in a traditional sense, is to work through the emotional release of this inherited memory. *Circumtrauma* acknowledges the lingering distrust and suffering that hinder identity, politicize memory, and define the relationships between those touched by the war.

VI. DIVINATION AS A WAY FORWARD: READING THE BODY'S LANGUAGE

My interest in divination, a global practice often used for sacred purposes and exemplified by geomancy's pattern-based meaning-making, lies not in the ritual but in its underlying logic of seeking understanding through patterns – a logic that informed my decision to shape the book through divination. It is crucial to create space for stories and acknowledge the negative emotions within them, recognizing their layers to seek understanding in the unknown, trusting that there's room for the stories we need to share.

Therefore, uncovering the layers of the novels I decided to use as source texts, I came to realize, required learning to read a story that is inherited by the way the body moves. I began to think of the cut-up as a way of divining a body of knowledge, a framework from which wisdom emerges from knowledge of what was and what may come. My cut-up method, by rearranging the 'patterns' of language from the war novels, became my way of 'reading' the enduring emotional landscape of the conflict.

Because my goal with *Circumtrauma* is to create an emotional release for this inherited memory, constantly shifting between interpretations, I turned to the Ifá divination system to deepen the meaning of the stories, written and oral, that I collected. At its core, the *Odu Ifá* operates on a binary system, generating 256 codes through the combination of two primary signs. I explored the binary structures within this work, as an aesthetic device and a framework for making trauma legible. For me, these codes felt like a way to remember, highlighting how memories shape the future. I love to think that we learn stories to make sense of what we know.

This binary nature is fundamental to the Ifá system. Think of it like a light switch with two positions, or the basic On and Off that underlie computer code. In standard binary numbers, these two states (often represented as 0 and 1) allow us to count. For instance, the decimal number 2 is represented as 10 in binary, signifying a Yes in the 2's place and a No in the 1's place.

Similarly, the Ifá Corpus is structured around two primary binary outcomes represented by Oyeku (often symbolized as 'O' or 'oo') and Okanran (often symbolized as 'I' or '|'). While Ifá doesn't directly use the numerical 1 and 0, its entire framework of 256 Odu arises from the permutations of these two binary possibilities across four positions. This creates a vast landscape of potential narratives and interpretations, mirroring the multifaceted and often binary nature of trauma itself: presence/absence, silence/speech, life/death. Inspired by this underlying logic, divination, specifically the Ifá Corpus with its inherent binary structure, provided a powerful framework for shaping the book, a way to divine the unspoken and, most importantly, to bear witness.

VII. THE STRUCTURE OF IFÁ: A MAP FOR THE UNSPOKEN

While Ifá divination is a complex system and a major source of knowledge in West Africa and the African diaspora, my focus here is on its foundational structure and how it informs my methodology. The *Odu Ifá*, a vast and ancient body of oral verses, operates on a binary system that generates 256 codes through the combination of two primary signs. This binary framework, which I explored as both an aesthetic device and a way to make trauma legible, offers endless possibilities for new narratives. It's important to note that the full spectrum of Ifá's properties extends beyond this binary focus, and misconceptions surrounding the system have unfortunately led to its negative perception in some communities. However, for *Circumtrauma*, my engagement centres on the structural implications of its binary logic.

My use of Ifá focuses on the structure of the first four main Odu. This foundational binary structure, where two elements combine to create a complex system of meaning, directly informed my approach to the cut-up method, allowing me to layer and juxtapose fragments of language to 'divine' the often-binary experiences of trauma – presence/absence, silence/speech – and bear witness to the unspoken. This binary structure, much like computer code, served as a way to 'read' the meeting of emotions as I cut up the novels line by line and mixed them with words from oral and digital sources. While the selection was arbitrary, the underlying binary framework of Ifá provided a structure for exploring the fragmented nature of narrating trauma, aligning with Ifá's capacity to hold multiple narratives.

VIII. THE SIGNIFICANCE OF FOUR: ROOTING THE CHAOS

Initially, my objective was to structure a poetry collection around the 256 permutations of the Ifá system. However, I quickly realized this exhaustive approach was both impractical and lacked a meaningful connection to the project's core concerns. The four sections of *Circumtrauma* align with the two-byte structure of Ifá divination poetry and, more importantly, serve to reveal the complexities and intensities of emotions within the context of the war.

Circumtrauma underscores the crucial role of emotions as carriers of memory, highlighting that genuine reconciliation necessitates a deep engagement with how narratives embody feelings about the war. Essentially, this systematized yet aleatory poetic method aimed to offer a deeper engagement with the unspeakability of trauma than mere representation.

Due to their randomness, the 'future' that emerges from these poems can be enlightening for understanding what emotion can do. 'Iwori,' for example, the nine-line poem in the final section, illuminates the anxieties of the past. There is a story lurking and a story being told that together attempt to elicit emotions associated with the death of a traumatized individual.

IX. INSPIRED BY THE FIRST FOUR: A FOUNDATION FOR DIVINATION

Drawing inspiration from the first four permutations of the Ifá divination system, *Circumtrauma* is structured into four sections. Each section contains sixteen poems, a number that reflects the binary system influencing their form.

The line count for each poem was determined by translating the binary figures of the divination process into decimal numbers. This structural approach, where the possibilities of cut-up poetry intersect with the inherent infinity of the binary system, mirrors the unpredictable ways trauma can linger and manifest as different forms of violence.

Ultimately, by employing the cut-up technique within this Ifá-inspired structure, *Circumtrauma* aims to evoke the wide range of emotions present in the chosen war novels and engage readers with the complexities of memory and the representational crises inherent in creating war stories that impact the future.

X. A CONVERSATION WITH THE PAST, GUIDED BY DIVINATION

Also, by employing the structure of the Ifá to creatively respond to the war using only words from the four novels, *Circumtrauma* aims to establish a close link with the orality of traditional African poetry, a form whose inventiveness arises from existing narrative 'texts.' Essentially, I pay particular attention to ensuring the poems resonate with the Ifá corpus rhapsodes while also erecting a complex understanding of the war narrative's dimensions in the reader's mind. This resulting intertextuality inherently disturbs the archive, highlighting the intricate relationships between the literary texts I borrowed and the new meanings they acquire in the poems.

Significantly, the meaning in found poetry emerges from my relationship with the source texts and my position as a poet, offering a chance to re/consider the coming together of words and their function in new contexts. For me, as a post-memory Nigerian writer, the weight of the war's literature and history informs this process of textual erasure and re-emergence. While contemporary writing often uses found poetry to explore complex past atrocities like post-colonial issues, racism, and other historical wounds through a present lens, allowing writers to narrate the silences within existing texts, my specific approach here focuses on the implications of using these novels as source material.

By adopting and rearranging the novels' exact phrases to convey new and distinct meanings, I leverage the arbitrariness of language, pushing the reading of unexpressed emotions to the fore through the surrounding context. These poems in *Circumtrauma* can thus be seen as a commentary on the complex emotions and the often inexpressible grief carried across generations and communities. Ultimately, the cut-up poems, embodying intertextuality, implicitly question the multi-dimensionality of the war and the deep grievances that shape individual and collective narratives.

XI. THE DIVINED PATH: SHAPING A BOOK FROM THE UNSPOKEN

Through *Circumtrauma*, I aim to give voice to the myriad memories of the Nigeria-Biafra War, exploring how its violence becomes normalized and fractures lives. The words we use carry potent emotions that evolve, shaping future memory. Ultimately, the path toward reconciliation lies in attending to these transmitted emotions, tracking and reimagining them. Or, to put it differently, acknowledging the violence that these words are capable of creating.

The decision to shape *Circumtrauma* through divination, specifically the Ifá Corpus, stems from its capacity to hold and interpret the fragmented silences inherent in inherited trauma. Just as Ifá interprets signs to understand the present and future, *Circumtrauma* uses the language and emotional weight within the war novels to 'divine' the war's enduring impact.

While the 256 Odu represent a vast landscape of potential narratives, my direct engagement focused on the structure of the first four. This framework, where the cut-up's inherent probability mirrors the unpredictable surfacing of trauma, also resonates with Ifá's oral tradition and my desire to amplify the many unspoken stories of the war. In essence, the Ifá Corpus provided both the structural and philosophical foundation for *Circumtrauma*, its binary logic informing the poems' form and its emphasis on interpretation mirroring my exploration of the war's unspoken emotional legacy. Divination, in this context, became a means to read the surrounding wounds, listen for the silent stories, and create a space for a different kind of remembering.

Circumtrauma is written for the memories of several voices waiting to speak their experience on the Nigeria-Biafra War, but it is also about the ways in which war violence gets normalized in framing interactions, such that it fragments ordinary lives; it is about the ways in which the words we read/use in our stories encapsulate emotions that take on new meanings in new contexts and become the memory of the future. This book, I hope, demonstrates how much the stories we tell, share, and carry about war regenerate trauma in new ways, ensuring that there are always unattended emotions from which social interactions are conditioned into unending questioning. The solution is to pay attention to the emotions transmitted in narratives and their circulation, to track and reimagine them as a beginning to the beginning of what could be a meaningful reconciliation.

PRIMARY TEXTS

Adichie, Chimamanda Ngozi. *Half of a Yellow Sun*. Vintage Canada Edition, Vintage Books, 2007.

Nwapa, Flora. *Never Again*. First Africa World Press Edition, Africa World Press, Inc, 1992.

Omotoso, Kole. *The Combat*. Heinemann, 1972.

Saro-Wiwa, Ken. *Sozaboy: A Novel in Rotten English*. Longman African Writers, Longman Publishing Group, 1994.

WORKS CONSULTED

Abba, A. Abba. 'Remediating Biafra: Adichie's *Half of a Yellow Sun* as a Symbolic Vehicle of Postwar Reconciliation.' *Research in African Literatures*, vol. 51, no. 4, 2021, pp. 1–17, https://doi.org/10.2979/reseafrilite.51.4.01.

Adebanwi, Wale, and Ebenezer Obadare. 'Introducing Nigeria at Fifty: The Nation in Narration.' *Journal of Contemporary African Studies*, vol. 28, no. 4, Oct. 2010, pp. 379–405. Taylor and Francis+NEJM, https://doi.org/10.1080/02589001.2010.512737.

Adebayo, Sakiru. 'Writing About the Dead in the Present Tense: *Half of a Yellow Sun* as a Work of Postmemory.' *Research in African Literatures*, vol. 52, no. 1, 2021, pp. 84–107. JSTOR, https://doi.org/10.2979/reseafrilite.52.1.06.

Adichie, Chimamanda Ngozi. *Half of a Yellow Sun*. Vintage Canada Edition, Vintage Books, 2007.

Alamu, F. O., et al. 'A Comparative Study of Ifá Divination and Computer Science.' *International Journal of Innovative Technology and Research*, vol. 6, no. 1, 2013, pp. 524–28.

Amoda, Moyibi. 'Background to the Conflict: A Summary of Nigeria's Political History from 1914 to 1964.' *Nigeria: Dilemma of Nationhood: An African Analysis of the Biafran Conflict*, edited by Joseph Okpaku, Third Press, 1972, pp. 14–75.

Anyaduba, Chigbo Arthur. *Writing Postcolonial African Genocide: The Holocaust and Fictional Representations of Genocide in Nigeria and Rwanda*. 2018 U of Manitoba PhD dissertation. https://mspace.lib.umanitoba.ca/bitstream/handle/1993/33534/Anyaduba_Chigbo.pdf?sequence=3&isAllowed=y.

Garba, Abdul-Ganiyu, and P. Kassey Garba. 'The Nigerian Civil War: Causes and the Aftermath.' *Post-Conflict Economies in Africa*, edited by Augustin Kwasi Fosu and Paul Collier, Palgrave Macmillan, 2005, pp. 91–108. Springer Link, https://doi.org/10.1057/9780230522732_6.

Maiangwa, Benjamin. 'Revisiting the Nigeria-Biafra War: The Intangibles of Post-War Reconciliation.' *International Journal on World Peace*, vol. 33, no. 4, Dec. 2016, pp. 39–67.

Mucina, Devi Dee. 'Story as Research Methodology.' *AlterNative: An International Journal of Indigenous Peoples*, vol. 7, no. 1, May 2011, pp. 1–14.

Neumann, Birgit. 'The Literary Representation of Memory.' *Cultural Memory Studies: An International and Interdisciplinary Handbook*, edited by Astrid Erll et al., de Gruyter, 2008, pp. 333–43.

Nwahunanya, Chinyere. 'The Aesthetics of Nigerian War Fiction.' MFS *Modern Fiction Studies*, vol. 37, no. 3, 1991, pp. 427–43.

Odoemene, Akachi. 'Remember to Forget.' *The Nigeria-Biafra War: Genocide and the Politics of Memory*, edited by Chima J. Korieh, Cambria, 2012, pp. 163–85.

Olusegun, Atere Clement. 'Ethnic Memory and Historical Injustices in Nigeria.' *Advances in Social Sciences Research Journal*, vol. 7, no. 5, May 2020, pp. 545–55. Scholar Publishing, 116.203.177.230, https://doi. org/10.14738/assrj.75.8340.

Omotoso, Kole. *The Combat*. Heinemann, 1972.

Onuoha, Godwin. 'The Presence of the Past: Youth, Memory-Making and the Politics of Self-Determination in Southeastern Nigeria.' *Ethnic and Racial Studies*, vol. 36, no. 12, Jul. 2012, pp. 2182–99. Taylor and Francis+NEJM, https://doi.org/10.1080/01419870.2012.699087.

Onwubiko, Emmanuel. 'Igbo Losses Counted at Oputa Panel.' *The Guardian*, 26 July 2001, http://www.hartford-hwp.com/archives/34a/051.html.

Oputa, Chukwudifu A., et al. *Synoptic Overview of* HRVIC *Report: Conclusions and Recommendation. 1, Human Rights Violations Investigation Commission*, May 2002, p. 98, https://hmcwordpress.humanities. mcmaster.ca/Truthcommissions/wp-content/uploads/2018/10/Nigeria.HRVIC_.Report-FULL.pdf.

Otiono, Nduka. 'Narrations of Survival.' *Wasafiri*, vol. 19, no. 41, 2004, pp. 70–71,

Oyewẹsọ, Siyan. *Perspectives on the Nigerian Civil War*. OAP Publications, 1992.

Royzman, E., et al. 'From Plato to Putnam: Four Ways to Think about Hate.' *The Psychology of Hate*, edited by R. J. Sternberg, American Psychological Association, 2005, pp. 3–35.

Sternberg, Robert, and Karin Sternberg. *The Nature of Hate*. Cambridge UP, 2008.

Truman, Sarah. E. *Feminist Speculations and the Practice of Research-Creation: Writing Pedagogies and Intertextual Affects*. 1st ed., Routledge, 2021.

ACKNOWLEDGEMENTS

Thank you to Coach House for providing a place for this poetry collection to call home. For being approachable and sensitive to my choices as a writer and an artist. I'd like to express my sincere appreciation to Nasser Hussain, James Lindsay, Crystal Sikma, and Alana Wilcox for their invaluable contributions that made this work possible. My thanks also go to Jazmin Welch for the original cover design. My deep gratitude to Edaoto for being supportive in sharing his practical knowledge on the Ifa divination system before I began to surf through books and materials. He emboldened me as a friend and an Ifa practitioner, to own it as a theoretical platform for reading what is beyond my understanding; that, really, is what the work is about.

Thank you to Akinola Olowookere; despite his involvement in research at the time I was working on this book, he provided me with a lesson in binary and a correlation as it applies to divination, and it informed my approach toward this project a great deal. Peter Midgley, for reading the early, early drafts of this work.

Given that this work began as part of my PhD project at the University of Alberta, I would like to express my gratitude to my absolutely supportive committee, who were overwhelmingly unwavering in their thoughtful comments toward this project. Teresa Zackodnik and Terri Tomsky, I can't thank you enough. Jordan Abel, my supervisor, who also became my editor, I appreciate your insights and belief in my approach. Your confidence that the work should reach the public is incredible, especially when navigating such difficult material.

Thank you to *South Parade* magazine for publishing some of these poems. I would also like to thank Peter Ton, my research assistant and student, who brought his coding knowledge and was incredibly helpful in ensuring I adhered to the aesthetics of using programming language, where I aimed for such. I would also like to express my gratitude to the Faculty of Art and the Department of English at Toronto Metropolitan University for their support in completing this project.

Above all, I am grateful to Eledumare! What's possible without the divine.

Jumoke Verissimo is a poet and novelist living in Toronto. She is the author of two well-recognized collections: *i am memory* and *The Birth of Illusion*, both published in Nigeria and nominated for various awards, including the Nigerian Prize for Literature. Her most recent novel, *A Small Silence*, received critical acclaim and was nominated for several awards, including the Edinburgh Festival First Book Award and the RSL Ondaatje Prize. It won the Aidoo-Snyder Book Prize. Her writing explores traumatic re/constructions of everyday life and its intersection with gender, focusing on themes of love, loss, and hope. She currently teaches in the Department of English, Toronto Metropolitan University.

Typeset in Albertan Pro and Iowan Old Style.

Printed at the Coach House on bpNichol Lane in Toronto, Ontario, on Zephyr Antique Laid paper, which was manufactured, acid-free, in Saint-Jérôme, Quebec, from second-growth forests. This book was printed with vegetable-based ink on a 1973 Heidelberg KORD offset litho press. Its pages were folded on a Baumfolder, gathered by hand, bound on a Sulby Auto-Minabinda, and trimmed on a Polar single-knife cutter.

Coach House Books is situated on occupied land, which is the traditional territory of several Indigenous nations, including the Mississaugas of the Credit (an Anishnabek people), the Haudenosaunee Confederacy, and the Wendat and Petun nations, and is now home to many First Nations, Inuit, and Métis people. This land is covered by the Dish With One Spoon Covenant, an agreement between different First Nations communities to share resources peacefully and equitably, and by the Two-Row Wampum, a covenant of mutual respect and non-interference between early settlers and the Haudenosaunee. The land is also subject to Treaty 13, sometimes called the Toronto Purchase, signed between the settler colonists and the Mississaugas of the Credit.

As a settler organization, we acknowledge that we have violated these treaties and agreements. We acknowledge the grievous and ongoing harm of colonialism, and we strive to work toward a future of justice and reconciliation.

Edited by Jordan Abel
Cover design by Jazmin Welch
Interior design by Crystal Sikma
Author photo by Cornelia Faith Photography

Coach House Books
80 bpNichol Lane
Toronto ON M5S 3J4
Canada

mail@chbooks.com
www.chbooks.com